Hand Over the Chocolate & No One Gets Hurt!

The Chocolate-Lover's Cookbook

Gloria Hander Lyons

Blue Sage Press

Hand Over the Chocolate & No One Gets Hurt!
The Chocolate-Lover's Cookbook

Inquires should be addressed to:
Blue Sage Press
48 Borondo Pines
La Marque, TX 77568
www.BlueSagePress.com

ISBN: 978-0-9802244-2-9

Library of Congress Control Number: 2008903451

First Edition: May, 2008

Printed in the United States of America

Table of Contents

Chocolate doesn't make the world go 'round, but it sure does make the trip worthwhile!

Hand Over the Chocolate & No One Gets Hurt

There's nothing more satisfying than a decadent chocolate dessert with its soothing, rich flavor that literally melts in your mouth.

For centuries, people from many cultures believed that eating chocolate instilled strength, health and passion in those who drank it.

The Spanish first discovered chocolate during the 16th century while searching for gold in the New World. They brought it back to Spain, where its popularity spread throughout Europe and then to the United States.

In 1519, Hernán Cortés claimed chocolate to be: "The divine drink which builds up resistance and fights fatigue. A cup of this precious drink permits a man to walk for a whole day without food."

Even today chocolate remains a symbol of love and devotion, presented as a token of our affection on holidays such as Valentine's Day and other special occasions.

Scientific research has revealed that chocolate is not the aphrodisiac once believed, but it does contain small amounts of a chemical called phenylethylamine (PEA), which is a mild mood elevator. It's the same chemical that our brain produces when we feel happy or "in love." Therefore, eating chocolate does produce a mild "rush" that makes many of us long for more.

Chocolate (particularly dark chocolate) was also found to contain flavonoids, which may have beneficial effects on cardiovascular health. They may also act as antioxidants, which are believed to prevent or delay certain damage to the body's cells and tissues.

I certainly don't encourage the use of chocolate for health food purposes, but nothing can compare to the satisfying indulgence of a sweet chocolate dessert to lift our spirits.

Let's not be greedy, though, and demand that others "hand over their chocolate". There's plenty of chocolate to go around—especially inside this recipe collection of delectable chocolate confections. It's the perfect cookbook for chocoholics everywhere.

I've gathered 78 of the most decadent recipes I could find. And because I don't like to work hard or wait long for my chocolate treats, these tasty concoctions are quick and easy to prepare.

But just in case you want to share your chocolate treasures, I've included a few fun ideas for chocolate theme parties, plus games, activities, decorations and guest favors.

Indulge yourself with chocolate!

Chocolate Beverages

Chocolate Mocha Punch

1-1/2 quarts water
1/2 cup instant chocolate drink mix
1/2 cup granulated sugar
1/4 cup instant coffee granules
1/2 gallon vanilla ice cream
1/2 gallon chocolate ice cream
1 cup whipping cream, whipped and sweetened to taste

In a large saucepan, bring water to a boil. Remove from heat. Add drink mix, sugar and coffee; stir until dissolved. Cover and refrigerate 4 hours or overnight. About 30 minutes before serving, pour into a punch bowl. Add ice cream by scoopfuls; stir until partially melted. Garnish with dollops of whipped cream.

Magic Potion Chocolate Punch

1/2 cup chocolate-flavored syrup
2 cups milk
2 (12 oz.) cans cola beverage, room temperature
Non-dairy whipped topping, if desired

In a 4-cup microwaveable measuring cup, blend chocolate syrup and milk. Microwave on high power 3-4 minutes or until hot. Divide chocolate milk into 8 mugs. Slowly pour about 1/3 cup of cola into each mug. Top with whipped topping if desired.

Coffee makes it possible to get out of bed, but chocolate makes it worthwhile.

Chocolate Tea

2 tablespoons black tea leaves
1 tablespoon cocoa powder
1 teaspoon dried grated orange peel
1/4 cup brown sugar, firmly packed

Add all the ingredients to a warm teapot, along with 6 cups of boiling water. Stir and then steep for 5 minutes. Stir again and strain into cups. Serve with milk and add additional brown sugar if needed.

Chocolate Rum Coffee

2 quarts brewed coffee
3 (12 oz.) cans evaporated milk
1 (16 oz.) can chocolate syrup
1/2 cup brown sugar, firmly packed
1 cup rum   Cinnamon sticks for garnish (optional)

In a Dutch oven, combine coffee, milk, chocolate syrup and brown sugar. Cook over medium-high heat, stirring occasionally, until sugar dissolves and mixture begins to boil; remove from heat. Stir in rum. Pour into mugs and garnish with cinnamon sticks. Makes about 20 servings.

Mocha Eggnog

1 tablespoon hot water
2 teaspoons instant coffee
1 quart dairy eggnog (or one 32 oz. can)
1/2 cup chocolate flavored syrup
1 cup whipping cream   Ground nutmeg

In a large bowl, stir instant coffee into hot water until dissolved. Add eggnog and chocolate syrup, stirring until well blended. Chill at least 2 hours. Just before serving, whip the cream until soft peaks form. Gently fold into eggnog mixture. Sprinkle with nutmeg. Makes 6 servings.

Decadent Hot Chocolate

1 cup milk
1 cup half and half
8 teaspoons granulated sugar
1 tablespoon brown sugar, firmly packed
1 oz. semi-sweet chocolate, chopped
1 oz. unsweetened chocolate, chopped
1/2 teaspoon vanilla extract

Place all ingredients except the vanilla in a saucepan and heat over medium heat until chocolate melts and sugar dissolves. Pour half of the mixture into a blender and process until foamy. Return to the saucepan, stir in vanilla and serve.

Rich & Creamy Hot Chocolate

1 cup milk
1/3 cup heavy cream
1/4 cup granulated sugar
5 oz. semi-sweet chocolate, chopped

In a small saucepan, heat milk, cream and sugar together until just boiling. Remove from heat and stir in the chocolate until melted. Serve warm in demitasse cups. Makes 4 servings.

There is a difference between hot cocoa and hot chocolate. The terms are often used interchangeably, but technically they are very different. Hot cocoa is made from cocoa powder, which is chocolate pressed to remove the cocoa butter. Hot chocolate is made from chocolate bars melted into cream. It is a richer, more decadent drink.

Chocolate Pastries & Breakfast Foods

Chocolate Kahlua Pancakes

1-3/4 cusp all-purpose flour
1/4 cup granulated sugar
3 tablespoons unsweetened cocoa powder
2 teaspoons baking powder
1/4 teaspoon salt
2 large eggs
1-1/3 cups milk
1/4 cup Kahlua
3 tablespoons butter, melted

In large bowl, combine flour, sugar, cocoa, baking powder and salt. In medium bowl, lightly beat eggs; stir in milk, Kahlua and butter. Stir egg mixture into flour mixture until smooth and blend thoroughly. Spray a large skillet with cooking spray or grease with vegetable oil. Heat skillet over medium-high heat. Pour about 1/4 cup of batter into skillet for each pancake. Cook 2-3 minutes or until holes appear on the surface and edges are slightly dry. Turn and cook 2-3 minutes until done. Transfer pancakes to plate and keep warm in a 200° oven until all batter has been cooked.

Chocolate Maple Syrup

1-1/2 cups maple syrup
1/2 stick (1/4 cup) butter
3 tablespoons unsweetened cocoa powder
Dash of salt

In a small sauce pan heat maple syrup and butter over medium heat until butter is melted. Add cocoa powder and salt, stirring until well blended. Serve warm over ice cream, pound cake, pancakes or waffles. Store in an airtight container in the refrigerator for up to 1 week.

Chocolate Chunk Scones

2 cups flour
1/3 cup sugar
1-1/2 teaspoons baking powder
1/2 teaspoon baking soda
1/4 teaspoon salt
6 tablespoons unsalted butter
1 large egg, slightly beaten
1/2 cup half-and-half
1 teaspoon vanilla extract
3 squares of semi-sweet baking chocolate, chopped

Preheat oven to 400°. In a large bowl, combine flour, sugar, baking powder, baking soda and salt. Cut in butter with a pastry blender until mixture resembles coarse crumbs. In a separate bowl, mix together egg, half-and-half and vanilla; stir into dry ingredients just until moistened. Stir in chocolate. Add a bit more flour if dough seems too sticky. Turn dough out onto a lightly floured surface; knead 8-10 times or until smooth. Pat into a 7" circle, about 3/4" thick. Cut into 8 pie-shaped wedges. Or roll dough to 3/4" thickness and cut out circles with a 2-1/2" biscuit cutter or a 1-1/2" cutter for mini-scones. Brush tops with milk and sprinkle with sugar. Place 1" apart on lightly greased cookie sheet. Bake for 18 to 20 minutes (15-18 minutes for mini scones) or until golden brown.

Chocolate Butter

1/2 cup unsalted butter, softened
2 tablespoons confectioner's sugar
2 tablespoons cocoa powder

In a small bowl, beat ingredients together until fluffy. Refrigerate until ready to serve. Soften for 15-20 minutes before serving.

Chocolate Cinnamon Rolls

1 (8 oz.) can refrigerated crescent rolls
2 tablespoons butter or margarine, softened
1/2 cup mini semi-sweet chocolate chips
2 tablespoons granulated sugar
2 tablespoons chopped pecans
1-1/2 teaspoons ground cinnamon

Preheat oven to 375°. Unroll crescent dough on a lightly greased surface; press dough perforations together to form a 7-1/2" X 14-1/2" rectangle. Spread butter over dough. In a small bowl, combine chocolate chips, sugar, pecans and cinnamon. Sprinkle chocolate chip mixture over buttered dough to within 1/2" of edges. Lightly press mixture into dough. Beginning at one long edge, roll up dough jellyroll-style. Cut into 1/4" slices. Place slices 1" apart in a greased 9"X13" baking pan. Bake 11-13 minutes or until lightly browned. Serve warm. Makes about 16 rolls.

Hot Mocha Breakfast Float

1/2 cup unsweetened cocoa powder
1/2 cup granulated sugar
1 quart milk
2 cups hot strong black coffee or 3 tablespoons instant
    coffee granules dissolved in 2 cups hot water
1 cup chocolate ice cream
Whipped cream & shaved chocolate, for garnish

In a large saucepan, stir together cocoa and sugar. Over medium heat, slowly add milk until well blended. Add coffee while mixing constantly. Remove from heat. Ladle into 6 (8-ounce) mugs. Top each with a spoonful of ice cream. Top with whipped cream and chocolate shavings if desired.

Brownie Nut Bread

1 (21.5 oz.) package brownie mix
1 (5.5 oz.) package buttermilk biscuit mix
2/3 cup water
2 large eggs
1/4 cup vegetable oil
1 teaspoon vanilla extract
1 (6 oz.) package semi-sweet chocolate chips
1 cup chopped pecans

Preheat oven to 350°. In a medium bowl, beat brownie mix, buttermilk biscuit mix, water, eggs, oil and vanilla until well blended. Stir in chocolate chips and pecans. Pour batter into 2 lightly greased nonstick 4-1/2" X 8-1/2" loaf pans. Bake 45-50 minutes or until a toothpick inserted in center comes out with just a few crumbs. Cool in pans on wire rack 10 minutes. Remove from pans. Cool on wire rack another 10 minutes. Slice and serve warm with Chocolate Cinnamon Spread.

Chocolate Cinnamon Spread

1 (8 oz.) package cream cheese, softened
3 tablespoons powdered sugar
2 tablespoons unsweetened cocoa powder
1 teaspoon ground cinnamon
1/2 teaspoon vanilla extract

In a small bowl, beat ingredients together until fluffy. Refrigerate until ready to serve. Soften for 15-20 minutes before serving.

Chocolate Banana Bread

1/2 cup butter or margarine, softened
1 cup granulated sugar
2 large eggs
1-1/2 cups all-purpose flour
2 tablespoons unsweetened cocoa powder
1 teaspoon baking soda
1/2 teaspoon ground cinnamon
1/2 teaspoon salt
1 teaspoon vanilla extract
1 cup ripe banana, mashed
1/2 cup sour cream
1/2 cup chopped pecans
1/2 cup semi-sweet chocolate chips

Preheat oven to 350°. In a large bowl, cream together butter and sugar until fluffy. Add eggs, beating well. In a separate bowl, blend together flour, cocoa, baking soda, salt and cinnamon. Stir flour mixture into butter mixture. Add vanilla. Stir in banana, sour cream, pecans and chocolate chips. Spoon batter into 2 greased and floured 8" X 4" loaf pans. Bake for 55 minutes or until toothpick inserted in center comes out clean. Cool in pans for 15 minutes on wire racks. Remove and cool completely on wire racks.

Cacao beans were so valuable in ancient Mexico that the Mayans and Aztecs used them as a means of currency to pay for goods and taxes.

Cappuccino Chocolate Chunk Muffins

2 cups all-purpose flour
1 cup granulated sugar
2 teaspoons baking powder
1/2 teaspoon ground cinnamon
1/2 teaspoon salt
1 large egg, slightly beaten
1 cup milk
2 teaspoons instant coffee granules dissolved in
   1 tablespoon hot water
1/2 cup butter or margarine, melted
1 cup semi-sweet chocolate chunks

Preheat oven to 375°. In a large bowl, blend together first 5 ingredients. Stir in egg, milk, coffee and butter; blend well. Stir in chocolate chunks. Spoon batter into greased muffin pan cups, filling each about 2/3 full. Bake 15-20 minutes or until done. Cool 5 minutes before removing from pan. Cool on a wire rack. Makes about 1 dozen.

Rich Chocolate Gravy

1-1/2 cups granulated sugar
3 tablespoons cornstarch
1-1/2 tablespoons unsweetened cocoa powder
3 cups milk
1 teaspoon vanilla extract

In a large saucepan, stir together sugar, cocoa and cornstarch. Slowly add milk. Cook over medium heat, stirring constantly, until mixture thickens. Remove from heat and add vanilla. Serve over hot buttered biscuits

---

A little too much chocolate is just about right.

Chocolate Peanut Butter Muffins

1/2 cup brown sugar, packed
1-1/2 cups all-purpose flour
1/2 cup unsweetened cocoa powder
2 teaspoons baking powder
1/4 teaspoon salt
3/4 cup semi-sweet chocolate chips
3/4 cup peanut butter baking chips
1/4 cup (1/2 stick) butter or margarine, melted
2 large eggs, slightly beaten
3/4 cup milk
1 teaspoon vanilla extract

Preheat oven to 400°. In a large bowl, blend together brown sugar, flour, cocoa, baking powder and salt. In a separate bowl, whisk together melted butter, eggs, milk and vanilla. Stir egg mixture into flour mixture just until moistened. Stir in chocolate chips and peanut butter chips. Spoon batter into 12 greased muffin cups. Bake for 18-20 minutes or until toothpick inserted into center comes out clean.

Each seed pod produced by the cacao tree is about the size of a pineapple and holds 30-50 seeds—enough to make about 7 milk chocolate bars or 2 dark chocolate bars.

Chocolate
Party
Treats

Chocolate Dipped Strawberries

8 ounces semi-sweet chocolate chips
24 large, ripe strawberries

Place chocolate chips into a microwave-safe measuring cup. Microwave on high for 30 seconds then stir. Repeat until chocolate is melted and smooth. Do not allow to boil. Make sure the strawberries are completely dry before dipping. If you use refrigerated strawberries, allow them to come to room temperature. Dip them into the melted chocolate. Set on waxed paper to cool. Refrigerate until ready to serve. Serve at room temperature.

White Chocolate Popcorn Balls

10 cups popped popcorn
1 cup chopped pecans
4 oz. white baking chocolate, coarsely chopped
1/2 cup butter or margarine
4 cups miniature marshmallows

Combine popcorn, pecans and chocolate in a large bowl. In a medium saucepan, melt butter over medium-low heat. Add marshmallows; stir constantly until marshmallows melt and mixture is smooth. Pour over popcorn mixture; toss until well coated. Dampen hands; shape mixture into 2-1/2" balls. Cool completely on greased aluminum foil. Wrap each popcorn ball in cellophane or plastic wrap. Makes about 1-1/2 dozen.

Dip it in chocolate; it'll be fine.

Chocolate Punch Bowl Cake

1 (18 oz.) pkg. chocolate cake mix
2 (4 oz.) pkgs. instant chocolate pudding
3 cups milk
1/4 cup Amaretto liqueur (optional)
10 Heath bars, crushed
32 oz. frozen non-dairy whipped topping, thawed

Preheat oven to 350°. Bake cake as directed. Cool completely, then cut into 1" cubes. In a mixing bowl, beat pudding and milk. Add Amaretto; set aside. In a small punch bowl, place half of the cake cubes. Top with half of the pudding mixture, covering all the way to edges of punch bowl. Spread half of the whipped topping over the pudding. Sprinkle half of candy over topping. Repeat with remaining half of cake, pudding, whipped topping and candy. Cover and chill several hours before serving.

Chocolate Mint Cheese Ball

1/2 cup semi-sweet chocolate chips
1/2 cup chopped pecans
1/4 cup of 1" diameter peppermint candies (about 9)
1 (8 oz.) pkg. cream cheese, softened

In a blender or food processor, finely grind first 3 ingredients. Stir mixture into cream cheese. Shape into a ball, wrap in plastic wrap and refrigerate until firm. To serve, let stand at room temperature 20-30 minutes or until softened. Serve with chocolate wafers.

Mini Chocolate Cheesecakes

Crust:
1 cup chocolate graham cracker crumbs
3 tablespoons sugar
3 tablespoons butter or margarine, melted

Filling:
2 (8-ounce) packages cream cheese, softened
3/4 cup granulated sugar
2 large eggs
1 teaspoon vanilla extract
1/2 cup semi-sweet chocolate chips

Preheat oven to 350°. Line 18 muffin cups with paper liners. Mix crust ingredients together and press about 1 tablespoon of mixture into bottom of each cup.

Place chocolate chips into a microwave-safe bowl. Microwave on high for 30 seconds then stir. Repeat until chocolate is melted and smooth. Set aside.

Beat cream cheese until fluffy. Add sugar, eggs and vanilla, blending well. Stir in melted chocolate. Spoon cream cheese mixture into cups; fill about 2/3 full. Bake for 15 - 20 minutes or until set. Cool before removing from pans. Cover and chill until ready to serve.

If chocolate is the answer, the question is irrelevant.

Chocolate Mint Brownie Bites

4 oz. unsweetened baking chocolate
1 cup butter or margarine
3 large eggs
1 cup granulated sugar
1 cup brown sugar, firmly packed
1 teaspoon vanilla extract
1 cup all-purpose flour
1/4 teaspoon salt
3/4 cup chopped nuts
2/3 cup chopped Andes® chocolate mint wafer candy

In a small saucepan, melt baking chocolate and butter over low heat. Remove and cool to room temperature. Preheat oven to 350°. In a large bowl, beat eggs and sugars until creamy. Stir in vanilla and melted chocolate mixture. Add flour and salt. Stir in nuts and chopped candy. Fill greased miniature muffin pans 2/3 full. Bake 15-20 minutes or until brownies begin to pull away from sides of pan. Cool completely before removing from pans.

Fudgey Chocolate Fondue

1/2 cup (1 stick) butter or margarine
1/2 cup unsweetened cocoa powder
3/4 cup granulated sugar
1/2 cup evaporated milk or light cream
1 teaspoon vanilla extract

Melt butter in small saucepan over low heat. Remove from heat and stir in cocoa. Add sugar and evaporated milk. Cook over low heat, stirring constantly, until mixture is smooth and hot. Remove from heat; stir in vanilla. Mixture will thicken slightly as it cools. Serve warm with pound cake pieces, marshmallows, cherries, pineapple chunks, strawberries, fresh fruit slices or other dippers of your choice. Makes about 1-1/2 cups fondue.

Chocolate Petit Fours

Petit Fours:
1 box (18.25 oz.) chocolate cake mix without pudding
1 box (3.9 oz.) chocolate instant pudding
3 large eggs
1-1/4 cups water
1/2 cup vegetable oil

Icing:
1-1/2 cups whipping cream
2-1/4 cups semi-sweet chocolate chips

For cakes, preheat oven to 350°. In a large bowl, combine cake mix, pudding mix, eggs, water and oil. Beat with an electric mixer on low speed until moistened. Increase speed of mixer to medium and beat 2 minutes longer. Pour batter into a greased and floured 10'X15" pan. Bake 20-25 minutes or until a toothpick inserted in center of cake comes out clean. Cool in pan 5 minutes. Remove and cool completely on a wire rack. Cut into 2" squares.

For icing, place cream in a medium saucepan; bring to a boil over medium heat. Remove from heat; add chocolate chips. Sir until chocolate is melted. Cool slightly. Place each cake square on a fork and dip into icing. Place on a wire rack with wax paper underneath to catch drips. Store in an airtight container in the refrigerator. Makes about 24.

Chocolate is nature's way of making up for Mondays.

Chocolate Cookies

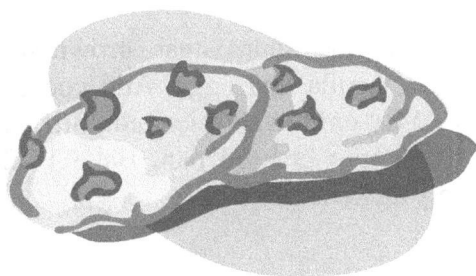

Mocha Fudge Brownies

1/2 cup unsweetened cocoa powder
1 tablespoon instant coffee granules
1 cup butter or margarine
1 cup water
2 cups all-purpose flour
1 cup granulated sugar
1 cup brown sugar, firmly packed
1 teaspoon baking soda
1/2 cup buttermilk
1/2 teaspoon vanilla extract
2 large eggs
1 cup semi-sweet chocolate chips

Preheat oven to 375°. Grease a 10"X15"X1" baking pan.

In medium saucepan, combine cocoa, coffee granules, margarine and water. Bring to a boil over medium-high heat, stirring occasionally; remove from heat. Cool slightly.

In large bowl, combine flour, sugar, brown sugar, baking soda, buttermilk, vanilla and eggs. Add cocoa mixture to flour mixture. Stir until well blended. Stir in chocolate chips. Pour batter into greased pan. Bake 15-20 minutes. Cool completely and cut into bars.

In 1896, the first recipe for chocolate brownies was introduced in the Fannie Farmer Cookbook.

Chocolate Meringue Cookies

2 egg whites
Dash salt
1/2 teaspoon vinegar
1/2 teaspoon vanilla
1/2 cup granulated sugar
6 ounces semi-sweet chocolate or chocolate chips, melted
    and cooled
3/4 cup chopped pecans

Preheat oven to 350°. In a large bowl, beat egg whites with salt, vinegar and vanilla until soft peaks form. Gradually add sugar, beating until stiff peaks form. Fold in melted chocolate and chopped pecans. Drop by teaspoonfuls onto greased baking sheets. Bake for about 10 minutes or until done. Makes about 3 dozen cookies.

No-Bake Chocolate Brownies

1 (14 oz.) can sweetened condensed milk
1 (12 oz.) box vanilla wafer cookies, finely crushed
1/2 cup chopped walnuts
1 oz. unsweetened baking chocolate, melted
1/2 cup semi-sweet chocolate chips, melted

In a large bowl, blend first 4 ingredients together; mixing well. Spread mixture into a greased 8" square glass baking dish. Spread melted chocolate chips over the top. Cover and refrigerate 1 hour or until firm. Cut into squares to serve. Store in an airtight container in refrigerator.

Among life's mysteries is how a two-pound box of chocolate can make a person gain five pounds.

Pumpkin Brownies

Brownies:
3/4 cup butter or margarine, softened
3/4 cup brown sugar, firmly packed
3/4 cup granulated sugar
1 teaspoon vanilla extract
1 cup canned pumpkin
2 large eggs
1-1/2 cups all-purpose flour
1/2 cup unsweetened cocoa powder
2 teaspoons baking powder
3/4 teaspoon pumpkin pie spice
1/4 teaspoon salt

Icing:
4 cups powdered sugar
1/3 cup unsweetened cocoa powder
1/3 cup butter or margarine, softened
1/4 cup boiling water
1 teaspoon vanilla extract

Preheat oven to 350°. For brownies: cream butter, sugars and vanilla in a large bowl. Beat in pumpkin and eggs until smooth. In a small bowl, combine flour, cocoa, baking powder, pumpkin pie spice and salt. Gradually add to creamed mixture; beat until well blended. Spread batter into a greased 10-1/2" X 15-1/2" jellyroll pan. Bake 14-16 minutes or until done. Cool in pan on a wire rack.

For icing, combine powdered sugar and cocoa in a medium bowl. Add butter, water and vanilla; beat until smooth. Spread on cooled brownies. Cut into squares and store in an airtight container. Makes about 3 dozen brownies.

Death by Chocolate Cookies

2 (8 oz.) packages (16 squares) semi-sweet baking
  chocolate, divided
3/4 cup brown sugar, firmly packed
1/4 cup butter or margarine, melted
2 large eggs
1 teaspoon vanilla extract
1/2 cup all-purpose flour
1/4 teaspoon baking powder
2 cups chopped nuts

Preheat oven to 350°. Coarsely chop 8 squares (1 package) of chocolate and set aside. Place remaining 8 squares of chocolate in a large bowl and microwave on HIGH power 1-2 minutes, stirring every 30 seconds until melted and smooth. Stir in butter, eggs and vanilla. Add flour and baking powder. Stir in chopped chocolate and nuts. Drop by 1/4 cupfuls onto ungreased cookie sheet. Bake 12-13 minutes or until cookies are puffed and feel set to the touch. Cool on cookie sheet one minute. Transfer to wire racks to cool. Makes 1-1/2 dozen.

Hell hath no fury like a woman who has sworn off fudge and chocolate.

Chocolate Truffle Cookies

4 oz. unsweetened chocolate, chopped
2 cups (12 oz.) semi-sweet chocolate chips
6 tablespoons butter or margarine
1/2 cup all-purpose flour
2 tablespoons unsweetened cocoa powder
1/4 teaspoon baking powder
1/4 teaspoon salt
1 cup granulated sugar
3 large eggs
1-1/2 teaspoons vanilla extract

Place unsweetened chocolate, 1 cup of chocolate chips and butter in a microwave-save bowl. Microwave on HIGH power until melted, stirring about every 30 seconds until smooth. Let cool. In a medium bowl, blend together flour, cocoa, baking powder and salt. In a large bowl, beat sugar and eggs about 2 minutes with an electric mixer. Beat in vanilla. Stir in chocolate mixture, then flour mixture until well blended. Add remaining cup of chocolate chips. Cover and chill until firm, at least 1 hour. Preheat oven to 350°. Shape dough into 1" balls. Place on an ungreased cookie sheet about 2" apart. Bake about 10 minutes, until puffed. Transfer to wire racks to cool. Makes about 4 dozen.

Easy Chocolate Peanut Butter Cookies

1 (16.5 oz.) roll refrigerated sugar cookie dough
36 miniature chocolate peanut butter cups

Preheat oven to 350°. Divide the cookie dough into 9 thick slices. Cut each piece into fourths. Place each chunk into a greased mini-muffin tin cup. Bake for 10 minutes or until lightly browned. Remove from oven and immediately push a chocolate peanut butter candy into the middle of each.

Chocolate
Cakes

Chocolate Cherry Nut Cake

2 cups all-purpose flour
3/4 cup granulated sugar
1 teaspoon ground cinnamon
1 teaspoon baking soda
1/4 teaspoon salt
2 large eggs, slightly beaten
1/2 cup vegetable oil
2 teaspoons vanilla extract
1 (21-oz.) can cherry pie filling
1 cup semi-sweet chocolate chips
1 cup chopped pecans

Preheat oven to 350°. In a large bowl, blend flour, sugar, cinnamon, baking soda & salt. Stir in eggs, oil & vanilla. Add pie filling, chocolate chips & nuts. Pour into a 10" greased & floured tube pan. Bake 55-60 minutes or until done. Cool 15 minutes on rack before removing from pan.

Molten Lava Cakes

6 (1 oz.) squares bittersweet chocolate
2 (1 oz.) squares semi-sweet baking chocolate
10 tablespoons butter
1/2 cup all-purpose flour
1-1/2 cups powdered sugar
3 large eggs
3 large egg yolks
1 teaspoon vanilla extract
2 tablespoons Grand Marnier

Preheat oven to 425°. Grease 6 (6-oz.) custard cups. Melt chocolate & butter in microwave. Add flour & sugar to chocolate mixture. Stir in eggs until smooth. Add vanilla & Grand Marnier. Divide batter evenly among custard cups. Bake 14 minutes. Edges should be firm but centers will be runny. Loosen edges with a knife and invert onto dessert plates. Top with vanilla ice cream if desired.

Chocolate Pound Cake

1-1/2 cups butter or margarine, softened
2-1/2 cups granulated sugar
5 large eggs
1 teaspoon vanilla extract
3 cups all-purpose flour
1/2 cup unsweetened cocoa powder
1/2 teaspoon baking powder
1/2 teaspoon salt
1 cup milk

Preheat oven to 325°. In a large bowl, cream together butter and sugar until fluffy. Add eggs, one at a time, beating well after each. Stir in vanilla. In a medium bowl, combine flour, cocoa, baking powder and salt. Add dry ingredients and milk alternately to creamed butter mixture, beating until well blended. Pour batter into a greased 10" tube pan. Bake 1 hour and 25 minutes or until a toothpick inserted in center comes out clean. Cool 15 minutes in pan. Remove cake and cool completely on wire rack.

A man found a bottle on the beach. He opened it and out popped a genie, who gave the man three wishes. The man wished for a million dollars, and poof! There was a million dollars. Then he wished for a convertible, and poof! There was a convertible. And then, he wished he could be irresistible to all women... Poof! He turned into a box of chocolates.

Mexican Chocolate Cake

4 (1 oz.) squares unsweetened chocolate
1/2 cup (1 stick) butter or margarine
1 cup water
2 cups all-purpose flour
2 cups granulated sugar
1 teaspoon ground cinnamon
1/2 teaspoon salt
1/3 cup buttermilk
1-1/4 teaspoons baking soda
2 large eggs, slightly beaten
1 teaspoon vanilla extract

Frosting:
2 (1 oz.) squares unsweetened chocolate
1/4 cup butter or margarine
8 tablespoons milk
4 cups powdered sugar
1/4 teaspoon ground cinnamon
2 teaspoons vanilla extract

Preheat oven to 350°. In a large saucepan, place 4 squares of chocolate, butter and water. Bring to a boil, stirring until chocolate is meted. Remove from heat. Stir in flour, sugar, cinnamon and salt; blending well. Add buttermilk, soda, eggs and vanilla; beating until smooth. Pour batter into a greased and floured 9" X 13" pan and bake for 25-30 minutes, or until the top springs back when touched lightly.

To Prepare Frosting: In a large saucepan, melt 2 squares of chocolate and 1/4 cup butter together. Add powdered sugar, milk, 1/4 teaspoon cinnamon and 2 teaspoons vanilla and beat well. Pour over warm cake.

Chocolate Zucchini Cake

2-1/2 cups all-purpose flour
1/2 cup unsweetened cocoa powder
1 teaspoon baking powder
1 teaspoon baking soda
1 teaspoon salt
1 teaspoon ground cinnamon
3/4 cup butter or margarine, softened
2 cups granulated sugar
3 large eggs
2 teaspoons vanilla extract
2 cups shredded zucchini
1/2 cup milk
1 cup chopped pecans

Chocolate Glaze:
2 cups powdered sugar
1/4 cup unsweetened cocoa powder
3 to 4 tablespoons milk, as needed
1 teaspoon vanilla extract

For Cake: Preheat oven to 350°. In a large bowl, combine flour, cocoa, baking powder, soda, salt and cinnamon. In a separate bowl, beat together butter and sugar until well blended. Add eggs, one at a time, beating well after each addition. Stir in vanilla and zucchini. Alternately add the dry ingredients and milk to zucchini mixture. Stir in nuts. Pour batter into a greased and floured 10" tube pan or Bundt pan. Bake 45-50 minutes or until a toothpick inserted in the center comes out clean. Cool in pan 15 minutes; turn out on wire rack to cool.

To Make Glaze: Mix together powdered sugar, cocoa, milk and vanilla. Beat until smooth. Drizzle over cake.

Hot Fudge Cake

This cake makes its own fudge sauce in the bottom of the pan while baking.

3/4 cup granulated sugar
1 cup all-purpose flour
1/4 cup unsweetened cocoa powder
2 teaspoons baking powder
1/4 teaspoon salt
1/2 cup milk
1/3 cup butter, melted
1-1/2 teaspoons vanilla extract
1/2 cup granulated sugar
1/2 cup brown sugar, packed
1/4 cup unsweetened cocoa powder
1-1/4 cups hot water

Preheat oven to 350°. In a large bowl, combine 3/4 cup granulated sugar, flour, 1/4 cup cocoa, baking powder and salt. Stir in milk, butter and vanilla; beat until smooth. Pour batter into ungreased 9" square baking pan. In a separate bowl, stir together remaining 1/2 cup granulated sugar, brown sugar and remaining 1/4 cup cocoa; sprinkle mixture evenly over batter. Pour hot water over top; do not stir.

Bake 35 to 40 minutes or until center is almost set. Remove from oven; let stand 15 minutes. Serve cake in small bowls, spooning sauce from bottom of pan over top. Serve with ice cream or whipped topping, if desired.

Flowers and champagne may set the stage, but it's chocolate that steals the show.

Chocolate Cola Cake

1 cup (2 sticks) butter
3 tablespoons unsweetened cocoa powder
1 cup cola beverage
2 cups all-purpose flour
2 cups granulated sugar
1/4 teaspoon salt
1 teaspoon baking soda
1/2 cup buttermilk
2 large eggs, slightly beaten
1 teaspoon vanilla extract

Frosting:
6 tablespoons cola beverage
3 tablespoons unsweetened cocoa powder
1/2 cup (1 stick) butter
1 (1 lb.) box powdered sugar
1 cup finely chopped walnuts (optional)
1 teaspoon vanilla extract

To Prepare Cake: Preheat oven to 350°. In a large bowl, blend together flour, sugar and salt. In a saucepan, heat butter, cocoa and cola until mixture comes to a boil. Remove from heat and stir into flour mixture. In a small bowl blend together buttermilk, eggs, baking soda and vanilla. Stir into flour mixture. Pour into greased 9"x13" pan. Bake 30 to 35 minutes or until done. Frost cake while warm.

To Prepare Frosting: In a large saucepan, heat butter, cocoa, and cola until boiling. Remove from heat and stir in powdered sugar, nuts and vanilla. Pour on top of warm cake.

Chocolate Turtle Cheesecake

2 cups of vanilla wafer crumbs
6 tablespoons butter or margarine, melted
1 (14 oz.) bag individually wrapped caramels
1 (5 oz.) can evaporated milk
1 cup chopped pecans, toasted
2 (8 oz.) packages cream cheese, softened
1/2 cup granulated sugar
1 teaspoon vanilla extract
2 large eggs
1/2 cup semi-sweet chocolate chips, melted

Preheat oven to 350°. In a large bowl, combine crumbs and margarine; press mixture onto bottom and sides of a 9" springform pan. Bake for 10 minutes. In a large saucepan, melt caramels with milk over low heat, stirring frequently, until smooth. Pour over crust. Top with pecans.

In a medium bowl, combine cream cheese, sugar and vanilla, beating at medium speed with an electric mixer until well blended. Add eggs, one at a time, mixing well after each addition. Stir in melted chocolate. Pour mixture over pecans. Bake for about 40 minutes.

Loosen cake from rim of pan; cool before removing rim from cheesecake. Cover and chill cheesecake until ready to serve.

The Greek term theobroma (the Latin name for cacao) means literally "food of the gods".

Chocolate
Pies

Chocolate Truffle Pie

11 squares semi-sweet baking chocolate, divided
1/2 cup whipping cream
4 large eggs
1/2 cup granulated sugar
1/4 cup all-purpose flour
1 cup frozen non-dairy whipped topping, thawed

Preheat oven to 325°. Grate 1 square of the chocolate; set aside. Place remaining 10 chocolate squares in a large, microwaveable bowl. Add cream. Microwave on HIGH 2 minutes or until chocolate is almost melted. Stir until chocolate is completely melted; cool slightly. Add eggs, sugar and flour; beat with wire whisk until well blended. Pour into lightly greased 9-inch pie plate.

Bake 35 minutes or until outer half of pie is puffed and center is slightly soft; cool. Top each slice with a dollop of whipped topping just before serving. Sprinkle with the grated chocolate if desired.

An average bar of chocolate contains about 27 mg of caffeine, about half the amount found in a cola and one third of the amount in a cup of coffee.

Impossible Chocolate Pie

1 cup milk
1/4 cup butter, softened
1 teaspoon vanilla extract
2 large eggs
2 (1 oz.) squares unsweetened chocolate, melted and cooled
1 cup granulated sugar
1/2 cup biscuit baking mix

Preheat oven to 350°. Grease a 9" pie plate. In blender or food processor, place all ingredients. Cover and process for 45-60 seconds until mixture is smooth. Pour into prepared pie pan. Bake for 25-30 minutes until pie springs back when lightly touched in center. Cool completely before slicing. To serve, top each slice with ice cream and chocolate sauce if desired.

German Chocolate Pie

1 unbaked 9" pie crust shell
1 (4 oz.) pkg. German baking chocolate
1/4 cup butter or margarine
3 large eggs, slightly beaten
1 (12 oz.) can evaporated milk
1/2 cup granulated sugar
1-1/2 cups sweetened, flaked coconut
1/2 cup chopped nuts

Preheat oven to 400°. In a large, microwave safe bowl, microwave butter and chocolate on HIGH power until melted, stirring every 30 seconds until smooth. Stir in eggs, milk, sugar, coconut and nuts. Pour into pie crust shell. Bake 25-30 minutes or until set. Cool completely before serving.

Chocolate Cream Pie in Butter Crunch Crust

1 (4-serving size) pkg. chocolate pudding mix (not instant)
2 cups milk
1/2 cup semi-sweet chocolate chips
1 cup whipping cream

Prepare Butter Crunch Pie Crust and let cool. Combine pudding mix, milk and chocolate chips in a large saucepan. Bring to a boil over medium heat and cook, stirring constantly, until mixture thickens. Cool but do not allow mixture to set.

In a large bowl, beat whipping cream until soft peaks form. Fold into cooled pudding mixture. Pour filling into Butter Crunch Pie Crust, sprinkle reserved crumbs on top. Cover and chill until set.

Butter Crunch Pie Crust

1/2 cup butter or margarine
1 cup flour
1/4 cup brown sugar, firmly packed
1/2 cup chopped pecans

Preheat oven to 400°. Mix all ingredients together. Spread in a 13" X 9" pan. Bake for 15 minutes. Remove from oven and stir. Save 3/4 cup mixture for topping. Press remaining crust mixture into 9" pie pan. Cool. Pour in filling and sprinkle reserved crumbs on top. Cover and chill until set.

Fudgey Microwave Pie

1 cup granulated sugar
1/2 cup butter or margarine, melted
1/2 cup all-purpose flour
1/2 cup chopped pecans
2 large eggs
3 tablespoons unsweetened cocoa powder
1 teaspoon vanilla extract

In a large bowl, combine all ingredients together until well blended. Pour batter into a greased 9" microwave-safe pie plate. Microwave on medium power (60%) 10 to 12 minutes or until almost set in center (do not over bake). If microwave does not have a turntable, rotate pie one-quarter turn every 3-4 minutes during cooking. Serve warm with ice cream and chocolate sauce if desired.

No-Bake Chocolate Cheesecake Pie

1-1/2 cups semisweet chocolate chips
1/2 cup granulated sugar
11 ounces cream cheese
1/4 cup butter or margarine, softened
2 cups frozen non-dairy whipped topping, thawed
1 (8" or 9") graham cracker crust (regular or chocolate)
Shaved milk chocolate for garnish, optional

Melt chocolate chips in microwave or over low heat in saucepan, stirring frequently until smooth and melted. Set aside to cool. In large bowl, beat cream cheese, sugar and butter until smooth. Stir in melted chocolate. Fold in whipped topping until blended. Spoon cheese filling mixture into graham cracker crust. Garnish with shaved chocolate, if desired. Cover and chill until firm.

Creamy Chocolate Pecan Pie

1 (8 oz.) pkg. cream cheese, softened
3/4 cup granulated sugar
3 large eggs
3/4 cup light corn syrup
1/3 cup unsweetened cocoa powder
2 tablespoons all-purpose flour
1 teaspoon vanilla extract
1/2 teaspoon salt
1-1/2 cups chopped pecans
1 unbaked deep-dish 9" pie crust shell

Preheat oven to 350°. In a medium bowl, beat cream cheese and sugar until fluffy. Add eggs, corn syrup, cocoa, flour, vanilla and salt; beat until well blended. Stir in pecans. Pour into pie crust. Bake 55-60 minutes or until a knife inserted in center comes out clean. If edge of crust browns too quickly, cover with a strip of aluminum foil. Cool on a wire rack. Cover and chill 2 hours. Serve chilled.

The average person in the U.S. today eats about 12 pounds of chocolate per year.

Chocolate Puddings, Parfaits & Toppings

Chocolate Bread Pudding with Caramel Sauce

Bread Pudding:
1 can (10) refrigerated buttermilk biscuits, baked according
    to package directions
2 cups milk
2 large eggs
2 tablespoons butter or margarine, melted
2 teaspoons vanilla extract
3/4 cup granulated sugar
1/4 cup unsweetened cocoa powder
1/3 cup semi-sweet chocolate chips

Caramel Sauce:
1/2 cup butter or margarine
1/2 cup granulated sugar
1/2 cup brown sugar, firmly packed
1/2 cup evaporated milk
2 teaspoons vanilla extract

To prepare bread pudding: Preheat oven to 350°. Tear baked biscuits into small pieces. In a large bowl, combine biscuit pieces and milk; set aside. In a medium bowl, beat eggs, butter and vanilla until well blended. Add sugar and cocoa. Stir in chocolate chips. Add chocolate mixture to biscuit mixture; stir until well blended. Pour into a greased 8" square glass baking dish. Bake 55-60 minutes or until set in center.

To prepare sauce: Combine butter, sugars and milk in a medium saucepan. Cook over low heat, stirring constantly until sugars dissolve. Increase heat to medium and bring to a boil. Cook, stirring constantly, about 9-10 minutes or until thickened. Remove from heat; stir in vanilla.

Cut warm bread pudding into squares and serve with warm sauce.

Black Forest Parfaits

1 (3.4 oz.) package instant white chocolate pudding
2 cups milk
1 (20 oz.) can cherry pie filling
3/4 cup chocolate wafer cookie crumbs
1/2 cup frozen non-dairy whipped topping, thawed

Prepare pudding mix according to package directions. Divide half of pudding evenly among 6 (6 oz.) parfait or stemmed glasses. Spoon half of pie filling evenly over pudding in glasses. Top pie filling evenly with half of cookie crumbs. Repeat layers with remaining pudding, pie filling and cookie crumbs. Top each serving with a dollop of whipped topping. Cover and chill until ready to serve.

Double Chocolate Satin Pudding

1/3 cup granulated sugar
2 tablespoons cornstarch
2 tablespoons unsweetened cocoa powder
1 teaspoon instant coffee granules
1/8 teaspoon salt
1-3/4 cups milk
1 ounce semi-sweet chocolate, chopped
1 teaspoon vanilla extract

Combine first 5 ingredients in a saucepan; stir to blend. Gradually add milk, stirring with a whisk. Bring to a boil over medium heat, stirring constantly until thickened. Add chocolate; stirring constantly until chocolate is melted. Remove from heat; stir in vanilla. Pour into a bowl; cover and chill 2 hours or until set.

Chocolate Tornadoes

2 cups frozen chocolate non-dairy whipped topping, thawed
2 cups milk
1 package (4 serving size) instant chocolate pudding mix

Spoon whipped topping evenly into 4 individual dessert dishes. Using back of spoon, spread whipped topping into bottom and up sides of each dish. Place in refrigerator while preparing pudding.

Pour milk into large bowl. Add pudding mix. Beat with wire whisk 1 to 2 minutes. Let stand 5 minutes or until thickened. Spoon pudding into dessert dishes that have been lined with whipped topping. Cover and refrigerate until ready to serve.

Chocolate Chantilly

1/2 cup sugar
4 (1 oz.) squares unsweetened chocolate, chopped
1/4 cup water
1 teaspoon vanilla extract
1 cup whipping cream

In a microwave safe bowl, combine first 3 ingredients. Microwave on HIGH power 1-1/2 minutes, stirring every 30 seconds, until chocolate is melted and mixture is smooth. Stir in vanilla. Let cool.

Whip cream until soft peaks form. Fold into chocolate mixture. Spoon into dessert dishes. Cover and chill 2-3 hours or until set.

Bailey's Cream Chocolate Pudding

1/4 cup granulated sugar
1/4 cup cornstarch
1-1/3 cups milk
1/2 cup whipping cream
1 egg yolk
1/3 cup Bailey's Irish Cream
3 ounces milk chocolate, chopped
Sweetened whipped cream, optional

Combine sugar and cornstarch in a medium saucepan. Pour in milk and stir to blend. Whisk in cream and egg yolk. Place over medium heat and cook, stirring constantly, for about 4 minutes or until mixture comes to a boil and thickens. Remove from heat and stir in Bailey's. Add chocolate and stir until melted. Pour into individual serving dishes. Let cool slightly, then cover surface with plastic wrap. Refrigerate for two hours or until chilled. Top with whipped cream before serving, if desired.

Crock Pot Chocolate Almond Rice Pudding

4 cups cooked white rice
3/4 cup brown sugar, packed
1/4 cup unsweetened cocoa powder
3 tablespoons butter, melted
1 teaspoon vanilla extract
2 (12 oz.) cans evaporated milk
1 cup slivered almonds

Lightly grease the inside of a 4-1/2 to 6 quart crock pot. Combine all ingredients in the crock pot, cover and cook on low for 2-1/2 to 3 hours, or until all liquid has been absorbed. Stir before serving.

Frozen Chocolate Delight

1 (4-1/2 oz.) package chocolate instant pudding
1-1/2 cups cold milk
1 cup frozen non-dairy whipped topping, thawed
7 graham crackers, coarsely crushed
1/2 cup miniature marshmallows
1/4 cup chopped salted peanuts

Prepare pudding according to package directions, but use 1-1/2 cups milk. Let pudding stand for 5 minutes to thicken, then fold in whipped topping, graham cracker pieces, marshmallows, and chopped peanuts. Spoon mixture into six individual custard cups or dessert dishes. Freeze for several hours or until firm.

Chocolate Whipped Cream

4 ounces bittersweet chocolate, chopped
1 cup whipping cream
2 tablespoons granulated sugar

Place chopped chocolate into a medium bowl. Pour cream into a small saucepan; stir in sugar. Bring to a boil over medium heat. Pour boiling cream over chocolate; stir until smooth and chocolate is melted. Cover and refrigerate for 4 hours, until thoroughly chilled.

Transfer mixture to a large bowl. Beat until soft peaks form. Refrigerate for about 1 hour before using. Makes about 1-1/2 cups. Keep in refrigerator for up to 2 days.

Chocolate Candy & Sauces

Quick & Easy Chocolate Fudge

1 (14 oz.) can sweetened condensed milk
1 (12 oz.) pkg. semi-sweet chocolate chips
1/2 cup chopped nuts
1 teaspoon vanilla extract
Dash of salt

Put all ingredients except nuts in a microwave safe bowl. Microwave on HIGH power 1-2 minutes, stirring every 30 seconds until chips are melted. Do not allow mixture to boil. Add nuts. Pour into a buttered 8" square pan. Cover and refrigerate until set. Cut into squares.

Cream Cheese Chocolate Fudge

2 (8 oz.) packages cream cheese, softened
1 (2 lb.) package powdered sugar
1 (12 oz.) package semi-sweet chocolate, melted
1/2 cup chopped nuts (optional)

Place cream cheese in a large bowl. Beat with an electric mixer, adding powdered sugar a little at a time until well blended. Add melted chocolate chips. Stir in nuts. Pour fudge into a buttered 8" square pan. Cover and refrigerate for 1 hour before cutting into squares.

**The first chocolate Easter bunny
was manufactured in 1890.**

Chocolate Pecan Pralines

2-1/3 cups brown sugar, firmly packed
1 (5 oz.) can evaporated milk
2 tablespoons butter or margarine, cut into pieces
1 cup chopped pecans
1/2 cup semi-sweet chocolate chips
1/2 teaspoon vanilla extract

In a medium microwave-safe bowl, combine sugar and milk; stir until blended. Add butter and microwave on HIGH power 1 to 1-1/2 minutes or until butter is melted. Stir in pecans. Microwave on high power 6 minutes; stir and microwave 3-4 minutes longer or until candy reaches soft ball stage. Test about 1/2 teaspoon syrup in ice water. Syrup should easily form a ball in water but flatten when held in your hand. Add chocolate chips and vanilla; stir until smooth. Quickly drop by heaping tablespoonfuls onto waxed paper. Cool completely. Store in an airtight container. Makes about 1-1/2 dozen pralines.

Chocolate Peanut Candy

1 (12 oz.) package semi-sweet chocolate chips
1 cup peanut butter baking chips
1 cup lightly salted peanuts
1/2 cup raisins

Place about 5 dozen paper candy cups on baking sheets. Melt chocolate chips and peanut butter chips in a medium saucepan over low heat. Stir in peanuts and raisins. Drop teaspoonfuls of candy in candy cups. Chill 30 minutes or until candy is firm. Store in an airtight container in a cool place.

Raspberry Fudge Balls

1 cup semisweet chocolate chips
1 (8 ounce) package cream cheese, softened
3/4 cup vanilla wafer crumbs
1/4 cup seedless raspberry jam
3/4 cup finely chopped almonds

In a microwave or heavy saucepan, melt chocolate chips; stir until smooth. Cool slightly. In a mixing bowl, beat the cream cheese and melted chocolate until smooth. Stir in the wafer crumbs and jam. Refrigerate for 4 hours or until firm. Shape into 1" balls; roll in almonds. Store in an airtight container in the refrigerator.

Chocolate Bourbon Balls

1 cup finely crushed vanilla wafers
1 cup finely chopped pecans
1-1/2 cups powdered sugar, divided
2 tablespoons unsweetened cocoa powder
2 tablespoons Bourbon
1-1/2 tablespoons light corn syrup

Combine vanilla wafer crumbs, pecans, cocoa and 1 cup of the powdered sugar. In a measuring cup, blend the Bourbon and corn syrup; stir into the dry mixture until well blended. Cover and refrigerate for an hour or more. Sift about 1/2 cup of powdered sugar onto a large piece of waxed paper. Shape small amounts of the dough into balls then roll in powdered sugar. Store tightly covered in the refrigerator. Makes about 3 dozen.

Chocolate Caramel Apples

12 wooden craft sticks
12 medium Red Delicious apples
3 (14 oz.) bags of caramels
6 tablespoons water
28 oz. semisweet baking chocolate, coarsely chopped
5 cups chopped pecans

Insert craft sticks into stem ends of apples. In a medium saucepan, combine caramels and water. Cook over medium-low heat, stirring constantly, until smooth. Remove from heat. Holding each apple over saucepan, spoon caramel mixture over apples. Cool completely on greased waxed paper.

In a small saucepan, melt chocolate over low heat, stirring constantly. Remove from heat. Holding each caramel-coated apple over saucepan, spoon chocolate over apple. Roll in pecans. Return to waxed paper to cool completely.

Chocolate Peanut Butter Spread

1-1/2 cups smooth peanut butter
1/2 cup semisweet chocolate chips, melted
1/4 cup butter or margarine, softened
1/4 cup powdered sugar
1 teaspoon vanilla extract
1 teaspoon instant coffee granules
1 teaspoon hot water

In a large bowl, combine first 5 ingredients; stir until smooth. Combine coffee granules and water; stir until coffee dissolves. Stir coffee into peanut butter mixture. Serve with cookies or crackers. Makes about 2 cups.

Espresso Chocolate Sauce

1/3 cup strong coffee
2 (1 oz.) squares unsweetened baking chocolate
1/2 cup granulated sugar
3 tablespoons butter or margarine
1/4 teaspoon vanilla extract

In a saucepan over low heat, cook and stir coffee and chocolate until melted. Add butter and sugar. Cook and stir until dissolved. Remove from heat and add vanilla. Serve over ice cream or pound cake. Makes 1 cup.

Chocolate Praline Sauce

2 cups brown sugar, firmly packed
1 cup dark corn syrup
1/2 cup butter or margarine
1 cup whipping cream
1 (6 oz.) package semi-sweet chocolate chips
1-1/2 teaspoons vanilla extract
2 cups chopped pecans, toasted*

In a medium saucepan, combine brown sugar, corn syrup and butter. Bring to a simmer over medium-low heat, stirring constantly. Cook 15 minutes or until sugar dissolves. Remove from heat. Whisk in whipping cream, chocolate chips and vanilla. Stir until chocolate melts. Stir in pecans. Serve warm over cake or ice cream. Makes about 5 cups of sauce.

*Toast pecans in a dry skillet over medium-high heat, stirring constantly for a few minutes until lightly browned.

Chocolate
Gifts

Chocolate Tea Mix

1/4 cup brown sugar, firmly packed
3 tablespoons instant nonfat dry milk
2 tablespoons powdered French vanilla coffee creamer
2 tablespoons unsweetened instant tea
1 tablespoon unsweetened cocoa powder

Blend all ingredients and place in a small zipper-type bag. Recipe makes about 4 servings.

To prepare: Microwave 1 cup of water (or 3/4 cup for stronger tea) on high power for 1 to 1-1/2 minutes or until hot. Stir in 3 tablespoons of mix.

Mocha Cappuccino Coffee Mix

3 tablespoons granulated sugar
2 tablespoons powdered coffee creamer
1 tablespoon unsweetened cocoa powder
2 teaspoons instant coffee granules
1/4 teaspoon ground cinnamon

Blend ingredients and place in a small zipper-type bag. Recipe makes about 3 servings.

To prepare: Microwave 3/4 cup of water on high power for 1 to 1-1/2 minutes or until hot. Stir in 2 tablespoons of mix.

Orange Spice Hot Chocolate Mix

1 cup instant nonfat dry milk
2/3 cup semi-sweet chocolate chips
1 tablespoon granulated sugar
1 teaspoon dried grated orange peel
1/2 teaspoon ground cinnamon

Place all ingredients in a food processor or blender and process until finely ground. Transfer to a small zipper-type bag. Recipe makes about 4-5 servings.

To prepare: Microwave 3/4 cup of water on high power for 1 to 1-1/2 minutes or until boiling. Stir in 1/3 cup mix.

Chocolate-Cinnamon Popcorn Spice

1/2 cup powdered sugar
1/4 cup semi-sweet chocolate chips,
    chilled & finely ground
1 tablespoon + 2 teaspoons unsweetened cocoa powder

Combine all ingredients. To serve: Melt 1/4 cup butter in a small saucepan over low heat. Stir in 2 tablespoons of spice. Pour over 3 cups popped corn. Stir well.

In 1939, the Nestle Company first introduced chocolate baking chips.

Chocolate Stirring Spoons

1 (12-oz.) pkg. semi-sweet chocolate chips
2 teaspoons melted shortening (optional)
35-45 plastic spoons
1/2 cup white chocolate chips (optional)

Line baking sheets with parchment or waxed paper. Place chocolate chips in a microwave-safe bowl; microwave on medium power for 2 minutes or until melted, stirring every 30 seconds. If needed, thin melted chocolate by adding shortening and stirring gently. Dip each spoon in chocolate mixture to cover the bowl of the spoon; place on parchment paper to set. Optional: melt white chocolate chips in a small microwave-save bowl. Drizzle white chocolate over chocolate covered spoons for decoration. Cool before wrapping individually in plastic wrap or cellophane, tied with a bow.

Chocolate Malt Coffee Creamer

2 cups instant hot cocoa mix
2/3 cup non-dairy powdered coffee creamer
2/3 cup malted milk powder
1/2 teaspoon ground cinnamon

Combine all ingredients. Place in a plastic zipper-type bag. Makes 3 cups. To prepare: Stir 2 heaping teaspoonfuls of creamer into 8 ounces of hot coffee.

Chocolate is cheaper than therapy and you don't need an appointment.

Almond Joy Brownie Mix in a Jar

1-1/2 cups granulated sugar
1 cup all-purpose flour
1/3 cup unsweetened cocoa powder
1/2 teaspoon baking powder
1/2 teaspoon salt
1 cup sweetened, flaked coconut, gently packed
1 teaspoon almond extract (optional)
1/2 cup chopped almonds

Pour sugar into bottom of a 1-quart canning jar. Tap jar gently on lightly padded surface on the counter to settle sugar. In a separate bowl, combine flour, cocoa powder, baking powder and salt. Pour flour mixture evenly over sugar. Tap jar gently on counter to settle. Toss coconut with almond extract. Sprinkle over flour mixture and press down gently to pack. Sprinkle almonds on top and tap jar gently on the counter to settle. Screw on lid and attach baking instructions.

Baking Instructions:
Preheat oven to 350°. Empty jar of brownie mix into a large mixing bowl and stir to blend. Add 1/2 cup butter or margarine, melted and 2 eggs, slightly beaten. Stir until thoroughly blended. Spread batter in a greased 9" square baking pan. Bake for 25-30 minutes or until done. Cool completely in pan then cut into squares to serve.

If at first you don't succeed, have a little chocolate.

Double Chocolate Muffin Mix in a Jar

1/2 cup granulated sugar
1-1/2 cups all-purpose flour
1/2 cup unsweetened cocoa powder
2 teaspoons baking powder
1/4 teaspoon salt
1-1/2 cups miniature chocolate chips

Pour sugar into bottom of a 1-quart canning jar and stir to level. In a separate bowl, combine flour, cocoa, baking powder and salt. Spoon flour mixture evenly over sugar. Spoon chocolate chips over flour mixture. Place lid on jar, close and attach baking instructions.

Instructions:
Preheat oven to 400°. Empty contents of jar into a large bowl and stir to mix. In a separate bowl, blend together 1/4 cup (1/2 stick) melted butter, 2 large eggs, 3/4 cup milk and 1 teaspoon vanilla extract. Add egg mixture to dry mixture and stir just until moistened. Spoon batter into 12 greased or paper-lined muffin cups. Bake for 18-20 minutes or until toothpick inserted into center comes out clean.

So much chocolate, so little time!

Chocolate
Theme
Parties

Chocolate Tea Party

Have a deliciously decadent Chocolate Tea Party for all things chocolate!

- Your invitation can be attached to a small bag of individually wrapped chocolates and mailed in a silver foil-covered box. Make sure the weather isn't too warm—you don't want your guests' treats to melt. Or, cut your invitation from chocolate colored card stock and write the party information using a silver paint pen. Glue on a border of silver-colored glitter for pizzazz.

- Cover your serving table with a chocolate-colored tablecloth or fabric and serve all your chocolate offerings on silver trays and tiered serving dishes. If you really want to get fancy, use a silver tea set for serving your chocolate tea.

- For true chocolate decadence, have a small chocolate fountain as your centerpiece. Cut up pieces of pound cake and fruit served on toothpicks to plunge into the flowing chocolate.

- Serve Chocolate Tea (page 5), Chocolate Chunk Mini Scones (page 9) cut out using a 1-1/2" biscuit cutter, along with Chocolate Butter (page 9), Chocolate Cheesecakes (page 18), and Chocolate-Dipped Strawberries (page 16).

- For a fun activity, give your guests a pen and writing paper. Ask them to write down as many chocolate items as they can think of in 1 minute. The guest with the most items wins a chocolate prize. Be sure to have some of your guests read their answers—they can be quite entertaining.

- Favors can be a bag of Chocolate Tea Mix (page 5) inside a pretty tea cup. You can find inexpensive tea cup and saucer sets at flea markets and garage sales. Place a bag of mix inside each cup, then place the cup and saucer on a square of tulle. Bring the corners of the tulle together and tie them with a pretty ribbon. Don't forget to attach the instructions for preparing the mix.

The world's first chocolate candy was produced in 1828 by Dutch chocolate-maker, Conrad Van Houten. He pressed the fat from roasted cacao beans to produce cocoa butter, then added cocoa powder and sugar.

Chocolate Brunch Party

- Your invitation can be cut into the shape of a pancake or attached to an inexpensive plastic spatula and mailed in a padded envelope.

- Serve Chocolate Kahlua Pancakes (page 8), Chocolate Butter (page 9), Chocolate Maple Syrup (page 8), Cappuccino Chocolate Chunk Muffins (page 13), Chocolate Dipped Strawberries (page 16), Decadent Hot Chocolate (page 6), and Chocolate Rum Coffee (page 5).

- For your party activity, have a pancake race. Prepare plain pancakes ahead of time for this event. Separate guests into two teams. Give each team a small skillet containing one pancake. Each team forms a line. The first contestant in each line holds the skillet with a pancake inside. When the start signal is given, each contestant runs or walks down to a certain point marked by a chair or other object, goes around it and returns to the line to pass off the skillet to the next team member. During their trip, each contestant must flip the pancake into the air and catch it in the pan 3 times. The first team to finish is the winning team. If the pancake is dropped, the contestant must start over. Have extra pancakes on hand to replace any that fall apart during the race.

- For favors, give each guest a package of Orange Spice Hot Chocolate Mix (page 55) in a mug. Be sure to attach the instructions for preparing the mix.

Chocolate Tasting Party

- Make this a formal event and attach the invitation to an individually wrapped piece of gourmet chocolate. Ask each guest to bring individually wrapped pieces of their favorite chocolate (Godiva, Ghirardelli, Hershey's, Dove's or any unusual brand or homemade recipe they like) to share with the other guests. Make sure you tell your guests how many to bring.

- Provide an elegantly draped "chocolate table" with fabric-lined baskets displayed artfully at various heights to hold the chocolates each guest brings.

- Use a variety of chocolate brands in your menu, like German chocolate in the German Chocolate Pie (page 37), Mexican chocolate in the Mexican Chocolate Cake (page 30), Reese's peanut butter cups in the Easy Chocolate Peanut Butter Cookies (page 26), Andes Mints in the Chocolate Mint Brownie Bites (page 19) or compare recipes using Ghirardelli versus Hershey's cocoa or baking chocolate. Label each dessert and chocolate brand.

- Have each guest describe the chocolate she brought, why it's her favorite, where she found it or how she made it and any unusual facts about it.

- Play the chocolate trivia game on page 64.

- For party favors, give each guest a Chocolate Stirring spoon (page 56) and provide small velvet draw-string bags to take home the sample chocolates each guest brought.

Chocolate Trivia Quiz (True or False)

1. The Swiss consume about 22 pounds of chocolate per person per year. True: The Swiss lead the world in chocolate consumption per capita.
2. The nation that consumes the most chocolate is Belgium. False: Americans eat about 12 lbs. of chocolate per person, per year, but because of its dense population it leads the world in chocolate consumption.
3. The scientific name for the cocoa tree, Theobroma Cacao, is derived from the Greek language and means "food of the gods." True.
4. Africa produces the most cocoa. True: African countries produce nearly double the amount of South American plantations.
5. Chocolate was first manufactured in the U.S. by Hershey. False: Chocolate was first manufactured in the U.S. by the John Harmon Company in 1765.
6. Saucers were invented in the mid-1600's by Europeans, specifically for drinking chocolate. True: Drinking chocolate was very popular in Europe and saucers were invented to prevent the liquid from spilling onto fine clothes.
7. Cocoa beans were once used as currency. True: When Cortés arrived in Mexico, he found the native Indians using the beans widely in trade.
8. Up until the mid-1800's chocolate was only available as a liquid for drinking. True: Fry & Sons Co. in England introduced the first solid eating chocolate in 1847.
9. The nation that produces the most chocolate is Switzerland. False: The nation that produces the most chocolate is the United States.
10. The word chocolate is derived from the language of the Mayan Indians. True: The beans we use today for chocolate products were called "chocolatl" by the Mayans.

Chocolate Ice Cream Sundae Party

- Your invitation can be in the shape of an ice cream sundae with the party details written inside. Or attach your invitation to an inexpensive ice cream scoop and mail in a box.

- Festive colors are in order for this event. Cover your serving table with a bright-colored table cloth. Hang colorful balloons and paper streamers from the chandelier over your table. Follow through with bright-colored napkins and serving dishes. Sprinkle colorful paper confetti around the tabletop for more pizzazz.

- Serve build-it-yourself ice cream sundaes. Provide attractive dessert dishes for your guests to create their own sundaes. Offer Mocha Fudge Brownies (page 22) for the base, 2 or 3 flavors of chocolate ice cream, Espresso Chocolate Sauce (page 52), Chocolate Praline Sauce (page 52), Chocolate Whipped Cream (page 46), chocolate sprinkles, chips or chopped chocolate covered nuts. Provide cherries for the top or, even better, chocolate covered cherries.

- For an activity, have your guests guess the number of chocolates in a jar. The closest answer wins the jar of candy. Or ask guests to write down their answers to the question: If you were a chocolate dessert, what would you be and why? Collect their answers, read them aloud and ask guests to guess who wrote each one.

- Guests keep their dessert dishes as favors.

Chocolate Movie Party

- Your invitation can be a small box of Junior Mints attached to your invitation, which is in the shape of a movie ticket. Mail in a padded envelope.

- Serve Chocolate Popcorn Spice (page 55) over popcorn, White Chocolate Popcorn balls (page 16) and mugs of Decadent Hot Chocolate (page 6), plus any other chocolate treats you like from the cookbook.

- Be sure to have plenty of comfortable seating for your guests, plus snack trays for munching party treats during the movie.

- Dim the lights and show your favorite chocolate movie. It can be a silly movie like "Willy Wonka & the Chocolate Factory" or "Charlie & the Chocolate Factory", more serious films such as "Like Water for Chocolate" or "Chocolat". For this movie, serve Magic Potion Punch (page 4).

- For favors give small bags of Chocolate Popcorn Spice Mix (page 55) and don't forget to include the cooking instructions.

Chocolate Murder Mystery Party

- Your invitation can be attached to a small magnifying glass and mailed in a box. If you like, have your guests come dressed as their favorite mystery sleuth.

- Serve Death by Chocolate Cookies (page 25) and any other chocolate treats you like, but label each dish on your serving table with a mysterious name, like Murderous Mocha Punch (page 4), Felonious Fudgey Fondue (page 19) or "Who Dunnit" Fudge Brownies (page 22). Add to the ambience by keeping the lighting in the room dim, and use candlelight throughout the space.

- For the activity, play a murder mystery game. Each guest draws from a bowl a folded piece of paper with the name of a person who was murdered (make up a name) written on the front and a message inside that says to look for a particular symbol (knife, rope, candlestick, axe, gun, bottle of poison) to find the murder weapon clue. These clues are taped around the room. Each guest will be searching for a different symbol. This clue will have the symbol on the front and a clue inside that says what the murder weapon was and another symbol that will tell them where the person was murdered (book for library, plant for conservatory, bed for bedroom, car for garage, etc.). Repeat the clue search for who committed the crime, using symbols for names (Pickle, Cherry, Hand, Rose, Glass, etc.)

- The last clue they find will lead them to their reward, the guest favor inside a bag (a chocolate treat, of course!)

Chocolate Halloween Party

- Wrap the invitation around a Tootsie Roll which is wrapped in the shape of a mummy using 1/2" wide white cotton fabric strips. Guests unwrap the "mummy" to find the invitation. Mail in a padded envelope.

- Use lots of Halloween decorations and serve Pumpkin Brownies (page 24), Magic Potion Punch (page 4) and other chocolate treats from the cookbook. Label them with spooky names.

- Have a costume contest. (Optional: have guests dress as their favorite chocolate: bar, cookie, M&M, cupcake, etc.) Give chocolate prizes for several categories: funniest, most creative, scariest, etc.

- Have guests search for their party favors. Wrap Tootsie Rolls in the shape of a mummy using torn strips of white cotton fabric (old sheets are fine; tear them about 1/2" wide). Enclose a small piece of paper inside with a hieroglyphic symbol printed on it. Each guest unwinds the mummy to find their symbol and match it to the symbol on a paper bag that contains a Chocolate Caramel Apple (page 51) inside a cellophane wrapper. Place these bags around the room so guests will need to search for the one that matches their symbol. Sample symbols are below:

Recipe Index

About the Author

Gloria Hander Lyons has channeled 30 years of training and hands-on experience in the areas of art, interior decorating, crafting and event planning into writing creative how-to books. Her books cover a wide range of topics including decorating your home, cooking, planning weddings and tea parties, crafting and self-publishing. She has designed original craft projects featured in magazines, such as *Better Homes and Gardens, McCall's, Country Handcrafts* and *Crafts*.

She teaches interior decorating, cooking, self-publishing and wedding planning classes at her local community college, as well as private classes and workshops. Much to her family's delight, her kitchen is in non-stop test mode, creating recipes for new cookbooks.

Check out her monthly newsletter for free craft ideas, decorating and event planning tips and taste-tempting recipes at: www.BlueSagePress.com.

Other Books by Gloria Hander Lyons

- *Easy Microwave Desserts in a Mug*
- *Easy Microwave Desserts in a Mug for Kids*
- *No Rules – Just Fun Decorating*
- *Just Fun Decorating for Tweens & Teens*
- *Decorating Basics: For Men Only!*
- *If Teapots Could Talk—Fun Ideas for Tea Parties*
- *Teapots & Teddy Bears—Fun Ideas for Children's Tea Parties*
- *The Super-Bride's Guide for Dodging Wedding Pitfalls*
- *Designs That Sell: How To Make Your Home Show Better and Sell Faster*
- *A Taste of Lavender: Delectable Treats with an Exotic Floral Flavor*
- *Lavender Sensations: Fragrant Herbs for Home & Bath*
- *Self-Publishing on a Budget: A Do-It-All-Yourself Guide*
- *The Secret Ingredient: Tasty Recipes with an Unusual Twist*

Ordering Information

To order additional copies of this book, send check or money order payable to:

Blue Sage Press
48 Borondo Pines
La Marque, TX 77568

Cost for this edition is $7.95 per book (U.S. currency only) plus $3.50 shipping and handling for the first book and $1.50 for each additional book shipped to the same U.S. address.

Texas residents add 8.25% sales tax to total order amount.

To pay by credit card or get a complete list of books written by Gloria Hander Lyons, visit our website:

www.BlueSagePress.com

www.ingramcontent.com/pod-product-compliance
Lightning Source LLC
Chambersburg PA
CBHW060657030426
42337CB00017B/2668